Jane Means Appleton Pierce

Jane Means Appleton Pierce

✳✳✳✳✳✳✳✳✳✳✳✳✳✳✳✳✳✳✳✳✳✳✳✳✳

1806–1863

BY DEBORAH KENT

CHILDREN'S PRESS®
A Division of Grolier Publishing
New York   London   Hong Kong   Sydney
Danbury, Connecticut

Consultants   *The Pierce Homestead, Childhood Home of Franklin Pierce*
The Hillsborough Historical Society
Hillsborough, New Hampshire

LINDA CORNWELL
Learning Resource Consultant
Indiana Department of Education

Project Editor: DOWNING PUBLISHING SERVICES
Page Layout: CAROLE DESNOES
Photo Researcher: JAN IZZO

Visit Children's Press on the Internet at:
http://publishing.grolier.com

Library of Congress Cataloging-in-Publication Data
Kent, Deborah
        Jane Means Appleton Pierce / by Deborah Kent
            p.   cm. — (Encyclopedia of first ladies)
        Includes bibliographical references and index.
        Summary: A biography of the wife of the fourteenth president of the United
States, who never wanted her husband to be in politics and who never recovered
from her grief over the deaths of all three of her children.
        ISBN 0-516-20478-5
        1. Pierce, Jane M. (Jane Means), 1806–1863—Juvenile literature. 2. Presidents'
spouses—United States—Biography—Juvenile literature. [1. Pierce, Jane M.
(Jane Means), 1806–1863. 2. First ladies. 3. Women—Biography.] I. Title.
E432.2.P54K46   1998
973.6'6'092—dc21   97–49629
[B]   CIP
                                                                    AC

Table of Contents

Jane Means Appleton Pierce

CHAPTER ONE

A Puritan Upbringing

✶ ✶ ✶ ✶ ✶ ✶ ✶ ✶ ✶ ✶ ✶ ✶ ✶ ✶ ✶ ✶ ✶ ✶

When Jane Means Appleton was thirteen years old, her father died. His death came as no surprise to his friends and family. For years, they had watched his slow decline. In a sense, he had destroyed himself.

Jane's father rose before dawn each morning, after only four hours of sleep, to kneel in prayer. He forced himself to turn away from the table at mealtimes, eating as little as possible. No one could persuade him to care for himself. By fasting and going without sleep, he believed he was obeying God's will. He deprived himself of rest and food until he developed consumption, or tuberculosis.

✶ ✶ ✶ ✶ ✶ ✶ ✶ ✶ ✶ ✶ ✶ ✶ ✶ ✶ ✶ ✶ ✶ ✶

The Reverend Dr. Jesse Appleton, a minister in the Congregational Church, was highly respected as a preacher but carried his religious beliefs to extremes.

The Reverend Dr. Jesse Appleton, Jane Appleton's father, was a minister in the Hampton, New Hampshire, Congregational Church. The Congregationalists were the descendants of the Puritans who founded the Massachusetts Bay Colony in the early 1600s. The Puritans were stern, sober people. They thought that earthly pleasures were sinful. They regarded dancing and fancy clothes as temptations of the devil. By 1806, when Jane Appleton was born, few Congregationalists were as severe as their Puritan forebears. But the Puritans had left their stamp on the people of New England. Compared to people in other parts of the country, New Englanders were still strict, serious, and pious.

When he was thirty-five years old,

Music performed by choirs was an important part of early New England religious services.

✧ ✧

Meriwether Lewis first glimpsed the Rocky Mountains on May 25, 1805.

In 1806, the same year Jane Means Appleton was born in Hampton, New Hampshire, Americans were wondering just how big the continent was. After all, settlement—including the seventeen states of the Union—extended only as far as the Mississippi River. What lay beyond? Few people had any idea how broad were the Great Plains, how tall the Rocky Mountains, or how far the Pacific Ocean. Few white people had seen the herds of buffalo that roamed the plains, nor the grizzly bears that ruled the mountains. And what native peoples lived in the unknown lands? To satisfy the national curiosity, President Thomas Jefferson had sent out a band of explorers led by Captains Meriwether Lewis and William Clark in 1804. In September 1806, they returned to St. Louis as heroes after a 7,700-mile (12,400-kilometer) trek to the Pacific Ocean and back. Loaded with maps, drawings, specimens, and journals, they described in detail, for the first time, the remarkable American West.

It seemed a good thing that the land rolled on forever because the population was booming. So many Americans were having children that people under sixteen

The Lewis and Clark Expedition reached the Pacific Ocean in November 1805.

made up the largest single group out of a population of 6.5 million. Families poured over the Appalachian Mountains to settle the fertile lands of Ohio, the newest state. Wagon roads crisscrossed the eastern third of the continent. Nearly everyone still lived on family farms. Industry was scarce, so the big cities were centers of trade and shipping. The ports of New York, Boston, and Philadelphia bustled with shipbuilding and the traffic of the great tall ships. But on the high seas, trouble brewed. England and France were at war with each other. The British were seizing American vessels and impressing American sailors. That is, the sailors were kidnapped and forced to work on British ships. By 1806, as many as 9,000 Americans had been impressed. Such violation of American neutrality would lead, eventually, to the War of 1812.

As Americans rejoiced in the freedom of their broad new land, slavery began to seem out of place. Black people comprised one-fifth of the population but few of them were free. In December 1806, President Jefferson appealed to Congress for a ban on the slave trade. Southerners and Northerners began to divide on the issue. The seeds of disunity that would come to full flower at the end of Jane's life were beginning to sprout.

Reverend Appleton was appointed president of Bowdoin College. Bowdoin was a small men's college in Brunswick, Maine. He moved to Brunswick with his wife Elizabeth and their six children. Reverend Appleton was highly respected as a preacher and as a professor of theology. He tried to set the best possible example for his students by living a pure, sinless life.

Yet, as the years passed, he carried his religious beliefs to extremes. He deprived himself so harshly that his health began to suffer. His friends grew concerned, then deeply worried.

Today, some people might say that Jane's father had some form of mental illness. Even the people who knew him felt that his behavior was abnormal. One fellow professor at Bowdoin

Jane's father was appointed president of Bowdoin College (above) when he was thirty-five years old.

New Hampshire, U.S.A.

☆ ☆ ☆ ☆ ☆ ☆ ☆ ☆ ☆ ☆ ☆ ☆ ☆ ☆ ☆ ☆ ☆ ☆ ☆ ☆

Jane Means Appleton was born in the small yet fiercely independent state of New Hampshire in 1806. The first colony to declare its independence from England in 1776, New Hampshire's motto proudly announces its determination to "Live Free or Die." (The saying still appears on state license plates today.) New Hampshire became the ninth state in the Union in 1788. Wedged between Maine and Vermont, this tall state touches Canada and the Atlantic Ocean, where it has only 13 miles (21 km) of seacoast. Nevertheless, New Hampshire thrived as a center of shipping and boat-building well into the nineteenth century. Eventually, some people moved inland to farm, and by Jane's day, textile manufacturing was just beginning in mills along the Merrimack River. Concord became the state capital in 1808. Then, as now, the state was heavily forested and more than 1,300 lakes watered the countryside. The White Mountains have always dominated the landscape. Mt. Washington climbs to the state's highest point, over a mile above sea level, at 6,288 feet (1,916 meters).

Amherst College (above) was founded in 1821, soon after Jane moved to the small town of Amherst, Massachusetts, where she spent her teens and twenties.

wrote that he showed a "morbid sense of responsibility for the religious and intellectual welfare of his students."

Life could not have been easy for Jane and her brothers and sisters. Their father spent most of his time praying, and he expected them to do the same. The children were not allowed to roughhouse or make noise. No one talked to Jane about the problems in her family. No one tried to comfort her. When Jane was growing up, adults did not talk with children about serious subjects other than religion. Children learned early that life was hard.

When Jane and her family moved to Amherst, it was a small town in the Berkshire Mountains surrounded by farms and woodlands.

Elizabeth Means Appleton, Jane's mother, belonged to a wealthy family of textile merchants. After her husband died, she took her children back to Massachusetts, where she had grown up. The Appletons settled in Amherst. Though it would soon be the site of Amherst College, it was a small town nestled in the beautiful Berkshire Mountains when the Appletons moved there. Surrounded by farms and woodlands, it was a lovely setting in which Jane could begin a new life.

☆　☆　☆　☆　☆　☆　☆　☆　☆　☆　☆　☆　☆　☆　☆

CHAPTER TWO

An Unsuitable Suitor

* * * * * * * * * * * * * * * * * *

During her teens, Jane Appleton lived quietly with her family in Amherst. She read, took long walks, and attended church services. Jane was a small, slender girl with large, dark eyes and a shining crown of black hair. She was shy with strangers, but young men admired her delicate beauty.

In 1826, when she was twenty years old, Jane met Franklin Pierce. Pierce had just moved to Northampton, Massachusetts, a few miles from Amherst. He was a recent graduate of Bowdoin College, where Jane's father had served as president. When he learned that the Appleton family lived nearby, Franklin Pierce

* * * * * * * * * * * * * * * * * *

In 1826, Franklin Pierce moved to Northampton, Massachusetts (above), only a few miles from the Appletons' home in Amherst.

decided to pay them a visit. Almost at once, he and Jane were drawn to each other.

Franklin Pierce grew up in Hillsborough, New Hampshire, the seventh in a family of nine children. His father, Benjamin Pierce, was an officer during the American Revolution. General Pierce later served as governor of New Hampshire for two terms. From an early age, Franklin Pierce was keenly interested in politics. He chose to study law at Bowdoin, hoping it would prepare him for a political career. After graduation, he continued his law studies under two judges in Northampton.

Jane's family was dismayed by her growing affection for the handsome

Franklin Pierce was born in this house in Hillsborough, New Hampshire.

Franklin's father, Benjamin Pierce (right), served two terms as governor of New Hampshire.

young lawyer. Pierce did not come from a religious family. To make matters worse, gossips whispered that his mother had died of drink. Franklin himself spent far too many evenings in Northampton taverns, debating politics with his friends. Jane's relatives warned her that Franklin Pierce would never be a suitable husband.

In 1827, Franklin Pierce opened a law office in Concord, New Hampshire (above).

After a year in Northampton, Pierce opened a law practice in Concord, New Hampshire. Concord was about 80 miles (129 km) away from Amherst, a long distance in the days before automobiles. Jane's family sighed with relief. At last, Jane's troublesome suitor was safely out of the way. But Franklin found every excuse to visit Amherst. When he was away in Concord, he and Jane exchanged long letters. Franklin's letters always began, "My dearest Jeanie."

Jane tried her best to be a good influence on Franklin. She encouraged him to go to church, and urged him to stay away from taverns. Jane feared that his love of politics would lead Franklin astray. She once exclaimed to a friend, "Oh how I wish he was out of political life! How much better it would be for him on every count!"

Franklin Pierce spent four years in the New Hampshire legislature, which met in the State House in Concord (above). During his last two years as a legislator, he was elected Speaker of the House.

Despite Jane's efforts, Franklin pursued his political ambitions. In 1829, he won a seat in the New Hampshire legislature. Four years later, in 1833, he was elected to the United States House of Representatives.

By now, Jane Appleton had grown from a shy young girl to a mature woman of twenty-eight. Most of her friends were long since married and had flocks of lively children. Jane yearned to make a happy home for a husband and children of her own. She hated politics as much as ever. But her affection for Franklin had ripened into love.

Gradually, Franklin wore down the objections of Jane's relatives. His

Franklin Pierce was elected to the United States House of Representatives (above) in 1833, but continued to practice law in New Hampshire when Congress was not in session.

future looked bright. He was in a fine position to support a family. He had known Jane for eight years, and she had won his unflagging devotion. On November 10, 1834, Franklin Pierce and Jane Appleton were married at last.

After the wedding, Jane moved to her husband's family home in Hillsborough, New Hampshire. She made few friends in Hillsborough. After two years, she was pleased to settle in Concord, where Franklin Pierce continued to practice law. But whenever Congress was in session, Pierce left New Hampshire for Washington, D.C. Jane

A Work in Progress

* *

The Washington, D.C., that Jane so disliked was indeed a diamond in the rough in the 1830s and 1840s. Construction plans for city streets and buildings had started and stalled over the previous twenty-five years. To make matters worse, the British had burned the capital during the War of 1812. By the Pierces' time, great buildings such as the Capitol and the White House were far from complete, and grand but unpaved boulevards were clogged with mud in the rain and dust in the heat. So unsanitary was the sewage system that the city fell victim to the dreadful cholera epidemic that ravaged the East Coast in 1832. Permanent housing was scarce, as few senators or congressmen stayed long in Washington. Instead, they lived and ate together in boardinghouses, most leaving their families in their home states during the short congressional sessions that lasted only from December to March. Nevertheless, the business of government went on, and theaters, newspapers, and society thrived. Eventually, the city achieved the grandeur it enjoys today.

The very shy Jane Pierce disliked Washington society and was never comfortable at parties and balls such as this one.

hated to be separated from her husband. But she disliked Washington society even more. She was still very shy, and she was never comfortable at Washington parties and balls. Besides, people in Washington seemed to talk of nothing but politics. Most of the time when Franklin went to the capital, Jane stayed behind.

Like most women of her time, Jane Pierce had been raised to be an obedient wife. She believed it was her duty to stand by her husband, no matter what course he pursued. At the same time, however, women were taught that men were morally weak. A wife must do her best to guide her husband down a righteous path. Jane Pierce saw politics as a corrupting force in Franklin's life. She determined to win him away from campaigns, elections, and hard-drinking companions. It was a hopeless struggle, but it would consume much of their lifetime together.

☆ ☆ ☆ ☆ ☆ ☆ ☆ ☆ ☆ ☆ ☆ ☆ ☆ ☆

CHAPTER THREE

Joys and Sorrows

☆ ☆ ☆ ☆ ☆ ☆ ☆ ☆ ☆ ☆ ☆ ☆ ☆ ☆ ☆ ☆

Jane begged her husband to leave politics. But Franklin Pierce was a man on the rise. In 1837, he won a seat in the U. S. Senate. Reluctantly, Jane went with him to Washington, but she remained in the background. If she had to attend a party, she refused to discuss politics with anyone.

The Pierces' first child, a boy, died in early infancy. In 1840, when she was thirty-four years old, Jane Pierce gave birth to her second son, Franklin Robert. A third boy arrived the following year. He was called Benjamin, after his grandfather, Benjamin Pierce. In 1842, Jane finally persuaded her husband to give up

☆ ☆ ☆ ☆ ☆ ☆ ☆ ☆ ☆ ☆ ☆ ☆ ☆ ☆ ☆ ☆

This silver locket contains a picture of Benjamin, called Bennie, Jane and Franklin's youngest son.

politics so he could stay at home with her and the children. Franklin Pierce resigned from the Senate without completing his term.

Jane was happy in Concord, caring for her two little boys. But in those days, there were no immunizations or antibiotics. Many children did not survive to adulthood. Jane worried constantly over the health of her sons.

In a letter to her husband, dated August 1843, she wrote, "Ben has been much troubled with worms and loss of appetite, and Frank seemingly much in the way of before you left. I have been up with him four or five times every night and felt that it was time to ask a doctor's advice. The weather has been exceedingly unfavorable to health, so damp and warm.

Franklin resigned from the U.S. Senate (above) in 1842 in order to spend more time with his family.

I wish Frank was with you. I think a visit of two or three days in fine weather would be a benefit to him."

Though Jane did her best to care for him, little Frank was never a healthy child. He died in 1844, when he was four years old. His death left Jane desperate with grief.

Sadly, the death of a child was a common occurrence in 1844. Jane was expected to bear her loss with courage. After Frank died, Jane's mother urged her to be brave and to find solace in her Christian faith. "The comforting belief that he [Frank] . . . has been received by his Savior is sufficient to

This building at 214 North Main Street housed Franklin Pierce's Concord law office.

check immoderate sorrow for the loss of a child so young," wrote Elizabeth Appleton to her grieving daughter. "My prayers are that this event may be sanctified to us all and lead us to a constant reliance on God and a cheerful, true submission in trust. . . . I can well understand that you will miss him everywhere, but I trust that no murmuring thought is ever allowed to take possession of your mind."

After losing her two eldest sons, Jane lavished all her affection on her youngest child, Bennie. She fretted endlessly over Bennie's health. In 1845, her husband took Bennie for a visit to Hillsborough. Jane wrote urging Franklin to "see that his feet do not get cold, and that he is well covered at night."

For four years, Franklin Pierce lived the peaceful life of a small-town lawyer. To please Jane, he steered clear of politics. In 1846, President James K. Polk offered him the position of U. S. attorney general, but Pierce declined. In a letter to the president he explained, "You know that Mrs. Pierce's health while at Washington was very delicate. It is, I fear, even more so now, and the responsibilities which the proposed change would necessarily impose on her ought probably in themselves to constitute an insurmountable objection to leaving our quiet home for a public station at Washington."

Jane had kept Franklin out of poli-

Our Neighbor to the South

☆ ☆

Before its conquest by Spaniards in 1519, Mexico had been the home of several rich cultures, including the Olmecs, Toltecs, Mayas, and Aztecs. Like the North American Indians, however, native Mexican populations were greatly diminished after the coming of Europeans. The Spanish ruled Mexico for three hundred years, spreading the Roman Catholic faith and the Spanish language throughout that vast territory. As they intermarried with native Mexicans, children of mixed descent called *mestizos* were born. Among the three ethnic groups—white ruling class, mestizo workers, and impoverished Indians—arose a rigid and cruel class system. Finally, on September 16, 1810, a ten-year uprising began that led to Mexico's independence from Spain. In the 1840s, when Mexico and the United States went to war over borderlands, Mexico extended all the way north into present-day Nevada. When it lost these lands north of the Rio Grande to the United States, Mexico assumed its present shape and size.

The Mexican War: Fast Facts

WHAT: A war to acquire Mexican territory for the United States

WHEN: 1846–1848

WHO: Between the United States and Mexican armies

WHERE: Battles fought as far north as present-day Los Angeles and south to Mexico City

WHY: American president James Polk had been unable to purchase California and New Mexico from the Mexican government and decided to take them by force.

OUTCOME: In the Treaty of Guadalupe Hidalgo, Mexico gave the United States the land it wanted, which included southern California and most of the Southwest, in exchange for $15 million. Fifty thousand Mexican soldiers and thirteen thousand Americans died in the conflict.

tics, but she could not keep him away from war. President Polk was eager to expand the territory of the United States. He coveted Texas, which had broken away from Mexico and had become an independent nation. When the United States tried to annex Texas, Mexico resisted. President Polk declared war on Mexico in 1846. When the Mexican-American

This map shows the vast tract of land ceded by Mexico to the United States at the end of the Mexican War.

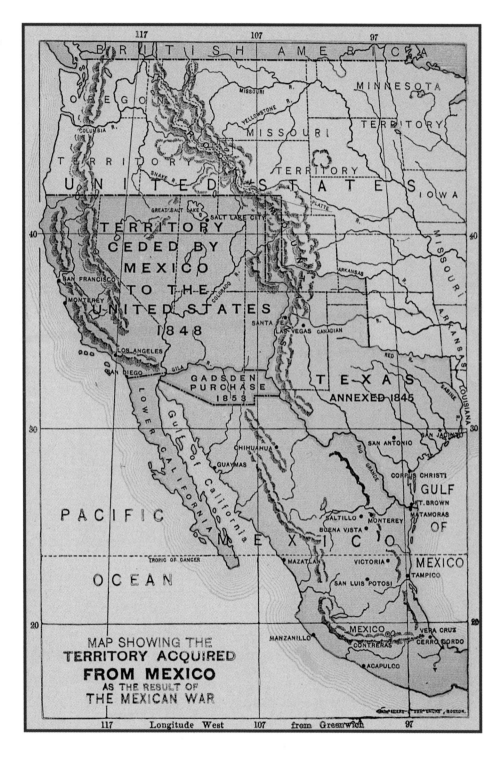

MAP SHOWING THE
TERRITORY ACQUIRED
FROM MEXICO
AS THE RESULT OF
THE MEXICAN WAR

In order to expand the amount of land owned by the United States, President James K. Polk declared war on Mexico in 1846.

War broke out, Pierce enlisted in the United States Army. He soon became a colonel and was ordered to lead a regiment into Mexico.

After being promoted to the rank of brigadier general, Franklin Pierce marched into Mexico under General Winfield Scott. During the Battle of Churubusco he was thrown from his horse and injured his leg. He did manage to avoid the bullets and tropical diseases that killed many of his men.

Winfield Scott (1786–1866)

★ ★

Born on his family's Virginia estate, strapping Winfield Scott stood six feet five inches (196 centimeters) tall, weighed 230 pounds (104 kilograms), and was the strongest man in the neighborhood by the age of nineteen. Although he studied law and passed the bar in 1806, he would devote his life to military service. As a young soldier, he was court-martialed for insulting a superior officer, so he spent a year studying foreign military theory. In an era when the American army was ill-trained and inefficient, he believed that smaller forces of well-trained soldiers could achieve more with less loss of life. He fought in the War of 1812 and the Indian Wars of the 1830s, rising through the ranks. In 1841, Scott was made general-in-chief of the army, where he did away with cruel punishments and overly harsh discipline. A stickler for details of dress and behavior, Scott won the nickname "Old Fuss and Feathers." In the Mexican War, he took the field himself after others had gained little ground and entered the capital of Mexico City within five months. Too outspoken and straightforward to make a good politician, he was never elected to serve as president, although he faithfully served all the presidents from Thomas Jefferson to Abraham Lincoln over his fifty-year career.

Winfield Scott was named general-in-chief of the army in 1841.

Franklin Pierce as a brigadier general during the Mexican War

During the Battle of Churubusco, Pierce was thrown from his horse and injured his leg.

To Jane's enormous relief, he returned safely.

The war with Mexico brought the United States a vast tract of land. The new territory included Texas and much of present-day New Mexico, Arizona, Utah, Colorado, and California. Soon, many more states would join the American Union. Most Southerners hoped that slavery would be permitted in those new states. Northerners generally wanted the territories to become free states, where slavery was not allowed. More and more, the issue of slavery split the nation.

Like many New Englanders, Jane Pierce felt that slavery was an evil that must be abolished. Franklin, too, disapproved of slavery. But he feared the growing division between the free North and the slave-holding South. He favored compromise if it might keep the peace.

As the election of 1852 drew near, the Democratic party looked for a candidate who could win votes in all parts of the country. A few party leaders suggested Franklin Pierce, the former senator from New Hampshire. Since Pierce was from New England, he would appeal to Northern voters. At the same time, his willingness to compromise on the slavery issue might draw votes from the Southern states.

Jane was horrified when she learned that her husband might become a presidential candidate. She implored him not to seek the Democratic nomination. Franklin promised

On September 14, 1847, General Scott and his troops entered Mexico City (left). Within five months, the Treaty of Guadalupe Hidalgo formally ended the war.

Jane Pierce with her son Bennie

that he would not pursue the nomination actively. He told her that he would accept it only if the Democrats really needed him.

At first, Franklin Pierce was not among the candidates whom the Democrats were considering for the presidential race. For a time, he seemed the least likely of them all. But at the nominating convention, delegates from the North and the South could not agree on a final choice. They went through thirty-eight rounds of voting. At last, the delegates were forced to compromise. The final nomination fell to Franklin Pierce.

The news filled Jane Pierce with dread. But she tried to be brave and make the best of the situation. "If what seems so probable is to come," she wrote to a friend, "I pray that Grace be given where it is and will be so much needed." If her husband should become president, she concluded, it would be a wonderful experience for Bennie. For Bennie's sake, she could endure anything—even life in the White House.

☆ ☆ ☆ ☆ ☆ ☆ ☆ ☆ ☆ ☆ ☆ ☆ ☆ ☆ ☆

CHAPTER FOUR

The Shadow in the White House

✯ ✯ ✯ ✯ ✯ ✯ ✯ ✯ ✯ ✯ ✯ ✯ ✯ ✯ ✯ ✯

Franklin Pierce was the Democratic candidate in the election of 1852. He ran against the candidate of the Whig Party, his former commander, General Winfield Scott. As the Democrats hoped, Pierce gathered votes from both the North and the South. He won the election by a landslide. Franklin Pierce would be the nation's fourteenth president.

The weeks after the election were filled with excitement. Jane bustled about, packing for the journey to Washington. She visited friends and relatives to say good-bye.

Shortly before the Pierces set out for the capital,

✯ ✯ ✯ ✯ ✯ ✯ ✯ ✯ ✯ ✯ ✯ ✯ ✯ ✯ ✯ ✯

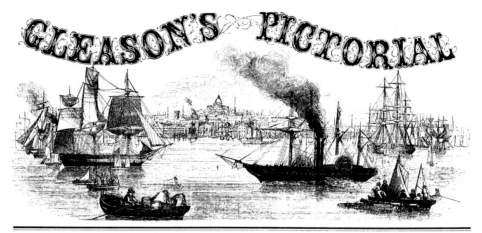

F. GLEASON, { CORNER BROMFIELD AND TREMONT STS. }   BOSTON, SATURDAY, DECEMBER 4, 1852. $2 PER VOLUME. } 10 CTS. SINGLE. } VOL. III. No. 23.—WHOLE No. 75.

PIERCE AND KING.

The President elect, of whom we give an admirable likeness below, by our artist Mr. Rowse, is a son of the late General Benjamin Pierce, of Revolutionary memory, and who was Governor of New Hampshire in 1827–29. The President elect was born in 1798, and is, therefore, fifty-four years old. He commenced his public career in the Legislature of his native State, and distinguished himself both as member and speaker of the House, until 1833, when he was sent to Congress as the Democratic candidate from his native district. While he was yet a member of the national House of Representatives, he was chosen by the State Legislature of New Hampshire a member of the United States Senate for the term of six years, in 1837. He remained until the year 1812, when he resigned his office,

and returning to his home, at Concord, devoted himself to the profession of the law. He was appointed first a colonel, and afterwards general, in the late Mexican war, wherein he distinguished himself for bravery and good generalship. After Mexico had been conquered, he resigned his commission, and returned once more to his home in New England, and to private life, from whence the late vote of his countrymen has elevated him to the highest post of honor in the world, for such we deem the Presidency of these United States. William Rufus King, Vice-President elect, was born in North Carolina, and is now about sixty-five years of age. Having, at an early period of life, taken up his residence in that part of the country which was afterwards known as the State of Alabama, he was elected one of the first senators of that State, when it

was admitted into the Union, and he took his seat in the body, over which he now presides, thirty-three years ago. He is, therefore, since Colonel Benton and Henry Clay are no longer there, the father of the American Senate. For a period of a quarter of a century, without interruption (1819 to 1844), he represented Alabama in the highest legislative seat on the continent. He was appointed, in 1844, to represent this country as ambassador at the Court of Louis Philippe. Since then his career, as a prominent member of the Democratic party, has been of a character to render him familiar to all. At the late (stormy) convention of his party, at Baltimore, he was chosen as the candidate for the Vice Presidency, in connection with Gen. Pierce as the Presidential candidate. The result is familiar to every reader of the Pictorial. As it

regards the likenesses given below, they are unquestionably excellent, and those who are personally acquainted with the gentlemen themselves, will bear willing and ready testimony to this.—Now that the election and the excitement which attended it have subsided, we can pause and admire the firmness and stability of our institutions which lead the masses off the battlefield of politics to the great plains of peaceful commercial pursuits, or other occupations, without a murmur, when the voice of the majority has been fully expressed. No bloodshed, no bullets (except paper ones), no riots; all is once more quiet, peaceable, *American!* What a contrast is here presented to the manner of doing things in the old world! There barricades and gunpowder would be the probable denouement of such a change of administration.

GENERAL FRANK PIERCE.   HON. WILLIAM R. KING.

This article about President-elect Franklin Pierce and his running mate William R. King appeared in Gleason's Pictorial, *a Boston illustrated newspaper.*

they attended the funeral of one of Jane's relatives in Andover, Massachusetts. Jane, Franklin, and Bennie went to Andover by train.

To Americans in 1852, the railroad train was an exciting modern invention. It enabled people to travel long distances at the unimaginable speed of 30 miles (48 km) per hour. But this new, high-speed transportation was sometimes dangerous.

After the funeral services, the Pierces boarded a train heading back to Concord. A few miles out of Andover, their car gave a sudden lurch. A fellow passenger, Reverend

Though the new railroad trains could move people long distances at fairly rapid speeds, train travel was sometimes a dangerous form of transportation.

Fuller, later described what happened: "I was looking out of the window when we felt a severe shock and the car was dragged for a few seconds, the axle of the front wheel being broken. In another second the coupling which joined our car with the other broke, and our car was whirled violently round so as to reverse ends, and we were swung down a rocky ledge. . . . I shall never forget the breathless horror that came over us during our fall. There was not a shriek nor an exclamation til the progress of the car, after having turned twice over the rocks, was arrested, having parted in the middle and being broken into many thousand fragments."

As he gazed around him, Reverend Fuller saw a woman huddled in the wreckage. "It was Mrs. Pierce, the wife of the president-elect," he wrote. "Near her in the ruin of shivered glass and iron lay a more terrible ruin, her only son, one minute before so beautiful, so full of life and hope." Twelve-year-old Bennie had been struck on the head by a flying chunk of metal. His skull was shattered, and he died instantly.

Jane was taken to a nearby house, where she collapsed in helpless tears. "I may not draw the veil from that picture," Reverend Fuller wrote. "Sacred is the holy privacy of sorrow, and the hearts of those who have suffered can feel what my pen may not describe."

The tragic loss of her last child was more than Jane could bear. No one could console her. To add to her misery, she learned that her husband had broken the promise he made before the Democratic Convention. The Democrats had not pressured him to run. He had sought the nomination, actively and eagerly. In Jane's tormented mind, Franklin's betrayal became tangled with Bennie's death. She blamed her husband for everything that had happened.

Desperately, Jane tried to understand why God had snatched Bennie away from her. At last, she thought she understood. God wanted her husband to dedicate himself entirely to his new responsibilities. Bennie would have been a distraction. The nation's welfare was at stake. How could she question God's will?

Inauguration Day loomed closer

Franklin Pierce's Inauguration Day parade in March 1853 moved up Pennsylvania Avenue toward the Capitol, where Pierce took his oath of office as president and delivered his Inaugural Address.

and closer, but Jane refused to leave for Washington. Her relatives urged her to go. They reminded her that it was her duty to stay beside her husband. "Duty" was a word Jane well understood. No matter what anguish she felt, she must do her duty.

Dressed in black, Jane and Franklin Pierce finally boarded the train for Washington. But when they reached Baltimore, Jane was overcome with dread. She got off the train and refused to go any farther. Her husband was forced to proceed without her. Jane did not attend the presidential inauguration. The traditional inaugural ball was canceled because the president and his wife were in mourning.

Crowds of onlookers witnessed Franklin Pierce take his oath of office as the fourteenth president of the United States.

Though Jane could not bring herself to appear in public during her first two years as First Lady, the White House public grounds were always filled with visitors.

For the first two years of his presidency, Franklin Pierce was forced to host White House dinners and receptions such as this one without Jane at his side.

When Jane Pierce reached the White House at last, she retreated to an upstairs room. She ordered that the public rooms of the mansion be draped with black crepe. Jane felt too sad to act as a hostess at parties and official receptions. Her aunt, Abby Means, took on the chores that usually fell to the First Lady.

For the next two years, Jane was lost in grief for her son. Alone in her darkened room, she poured out her heart to him in long, tortured letters. Once, she called in the Fox sisters, famous mediums of the day. The sisters claimed they had psychic powers and could communicate with the dead. They held a seance so that Jane could try to speak with Bennie.

This gown was worn by Jane Pierce during the time she was First Lady.

The Hydesville Rappers

✫ ✫

In 1848, the strange talents of sisters Margaret and Kate Fox, of Hydesville, New York, captured the country's attention. The Foxes claimed that the unexplained knocking sounds that occurred around them were messages from spirits. Their older sister, Mrs. Leah Fish, arranged large gatherings (at the price of $1 per person) and private seances where participants hoped to communicate with dead loved ones. Without fail, the rappings began, and the girls would translate. The fad—known as spiritualism—spread like wildfire. Spirits were soon communicating with believers in a variety of ways. They delivered their messages "from the other side" through human "mediums." In a trance, mediums wrote or spoke, played instruments, and moved tables. Arthur Conan Doyle, creator of that great skeptic, Sherlock Holmes, was a famous follower of spiritualism. The great magician

Harry Houdini, although hoping to contact his own dead mother, exposed mediums whom he believed employed the tricks of his own trade. And Mrs. Pierce was not the only First Lady to turn to spiritualism. Julia Tyler once held a party to contact the spirit world. Mary Todd Lincoln enlisted the Fox sisters to communicate with President Lincoln. (While living, Lincoln once said of seances: "For those who like that sort of thing I should think that is just about the sort of thing they would like.") In 1888, Margaret Fox admitted her fraud before a large audience. Taking off her shoe, she revealed that cracking the joint of her big toe made the knocking sounds. Her sister Kate fessed up later.

Weeds and Weepers

✱ ✱

Although Jane Pierce's mourning for her son was extreme, manners of her day did dictate fashion and behavior following the death of a loved one. Women, children, and even babies in the strictest households, dressed in mourning clothes, while men generally didn't bother with anything more than a black armband or black streamers, called "weepers," on their top hats. A widow mourned, officially, for two and a half years after losing her husband. For one year and a day, called first or deep mourning, she wore dresses of black crepe, a dull, crinkly fabric. For nine months of second mourning, she could add more elaborate trim. In ordinary mourning, which lasted three months, she might adopt livelier fabrics—still black—such as silk and lace. Finally, for six months of half-mourning, she could wear gray, white, lavender, or violet fabrics. The death of a son or daughter required eighteen months of mourning, six for a brother or sister, and six weeks for a first cousin. And, while a mourning widow could not remarry, a widower could do so whenever he chose. His new wife was then expected to wear mourning "weeds" (dresses) for her predecessor!

Jane did not appear in public until Pierce had been president for nearly two years. At first, she attended a few White House dinners with congressmen and foreign diplomats. She was still deeply depressed, and these public gatherings were agony for her.

Bennie was always in Jane's thoughts. In a letter to her sister, she wrote, "The last two nights my dear boy has been in my dreams with peculiar vividness. May God forgive this aching yearning that I feel so much. Mr. Pierce is burdened with cares and perplexities. He has had three large dinners, at all of which I have

Wondering about the Whigs?

★ ★ ★ ★ ★ ★ ★ ★ ★ ★ ★ ★

The Whigs and the Democrats were the two dominant political parties in the United States between 1836 and 1852. The word *Whig* comes from the Scottish Whiggamores, a group that opposed royal rule in seventeenth-century Scotland. In England, it came to stand for those people who were against a king with too much power. During the American Revolution, patriots who opposed British rule were known as Whigs. In the 1830s, a party calling themselves Whigs gained popularity in reaction to President Andrew Jackson, whom they believed had taken on too much power. They referred to him as King Andrew. They also believed in a strong federal government instead of powerful states. Four Whigs served as president. The two who were elected, William Henry Harrison in 1840 and Zachary Taylor in 1848, both coincidentally died in office of natural causes. They were both succeeded by their Whig vice presidents. The Whig Party divided and collapsed over the issue of slavery in the 1850s.

William Henry Harrison

Zachary Taylor

appeared, but not at the evening receptions. Little interruptions are very abundant here, and I do not accomplish half I wish to, either in reading or in writing. I came accidentally upon some of my precious child's things, but I was obliged to turn and seem interested in other things."

Jane Pierce's grief cast a feeling of gloom over the first years of her husband's presidency. It was nearly impossible for White House visitors to be cheerful in rooms that were shrouded with black cloth.

Jane was rarely seen, but her brooding presence made itself known. The people of Washington began to call her the "shadow in the White House."

☆ ☆ ☆ ☆ ☆ ☆ ☆ ☆ ☆ ☆ ☆ ☆ ☆ ☆ ☆

CHAPTER FIVE

Into the Light

✶ ✶ ✶ ✶ ✶ ✶ ✶ ✶ ✶ ✶ ✶ ✶ ✶ ✶ ✶ ✶

After two years in the White House, Jane Pierce gradually emerged from her seclusion. She appeared more and more often at banquets and receptions. She even helped to plan a few White House events.

As time slowly healed her grief, Jane began to enjoy friendships old and new. Writer Nathaniel Hawthorne had been a close friend of Franklin Pierce since they had met years before at Bowdoin College. In 1853, Hawthorne visited Washington and revived his friendship with the Pierces. Sometimes he took Jane for pleasant boat rides on the Potomac River. Jane had a

✶ ✶ ✶ ✶ ✶ ✶ ✶ ✶ ✶ ✶ ✶ ✶ ✶ ✶ ✶ ✶

Nathaniel Hawthorne had this portrait painted as a gift for his close friend Franklin Pierce.

lifelong love of literature. She and Hawthorne talked about books, including the writer's latest efforts.

Jane also made friends with Varina Davis. Varina was the wife of Jefferson Davis, Pierce's secretary of war. During the years Jane spent in her upstairs room, Varina's home had become the center of Washington's social life. Now Jane and Varina went for long carriage rides through the countryside of Maryland and Virginia.

Jane was still deeply religious. She attended church faithfully, and urged

During Nathaniel Hawthorne's 1853 visit to the Pierces, he sometimes took Jane for pleasant boat rides on the Potomac River.

61

Nathaniel Hawthorne (1804–1864)

✫ ✫ ✫ ✫ ✫ ✫ ✫ ✫ ✫ ✫ ✫ ✫ ✫ ✫ ✫ ✫ ✫ ✫ ✫ ✫

Nathaniel Hawthorne was one of America's most important writers. Often using the history of New England and drawing on his own ancestors' lives, Hawthorne wrote novels, such as *The House of Seven Gables,* which were famous for their dark symbolism and spooky scenes. His most famous work is *The Scarlet Letter.* For young readers, he adapted classical myths in *A Wonderbook for Girls and Boys,* which children still enjoy today. Hawthorne was born in Salem, Massachusetts, on July 4, 1804, and was raised by his mother after his sea captain father died in a

distant port. Hawthorne and Franklin Pierce had become friends at college, and when Pierce was nominated for president, Hawthorne wrote his campaign biography. After winning the election, Pierce appointed his friend to a diplomatic post in England. From that experience came Hawthorne's last book, which he dedicated to Pierce against the wishes of his publisher, who feared the president's unpopularity might affect sales. Greatly distressed by the Civil War, Hawthorne was in failing health when he last visited Pierce in Concord. On a weekend excursion through the mountains with his old friend, Hawthorne died in his sleep.

Nathaniel Hawthorne in his later years

During the time Jane spent in an upstairs room of the White House, the home of President Pierce's secretary of war Jefferson Davis and his wife Varina (above) became the center of Washington's social life.

everyone else to do the same. "Many a time have I gone from respect to her," wrote President Pierce's private secretary, "when left to my own choice I should have remained in the house." When he returned from church, Jane would often ask him about the sermon, just to make sure he had paid attention.

One morning in 1854, Jane Pierce set out in a carriage from the White House. She rode to the Capitol 1 mile

Varina Howell Davis (1826–1906)

✮ ✮

Little did Tennessee beauty Varina Howell know when she married Jefferson Davis, a Mississippi planter, that she would someday become America's "other" First Lady. During Franklin Pierce's presidency, both Davises were at the peak of their success. As secretary of war, Jefferson saw himself achieving his dream of fame as a soldier. The outgoing Varina ruled Washington society. By the eve of the Civil War in 1861, Jefferson Davis was a senator, but resigned his post when the Southern states left the Union. He was quickly elected president of the new nation formed by the Southern states, which was called the Confederacy. Its capital was Richmond, Virginia. As her husband attempted to lead the South through the Civil War, Varina faced criticism from Richmond society. With the defeat of the South came capture and imprisonment for Jefferson. Varina fought for her husband's freedom but won only the right to share his prison quarters. After his release in 1867, the family suffered more tragedy when two of their sons died of disease. Only when a friend opened her estate to them did Jefferson and Varina resume a normal life, and she helped him write his *Rise and Fall of the Confederate Government*. After Jefferson's death, Varina wrote a memoir of his life.

(1.6 km) away. There, she took a seat in the visitors' gallery to watch the debates in Congress. Washington society was astonished. It was well known that Mrs. Pierce hated politics. Yet there she was, sitting quietly in the gallery, listening intently through the endless discussions about domestic and foreign policy. What had come over the First Lady? Why had she changed?

From that day on, Jane attended congressional sessions regularly. No one knows for certain what transformed her attitude toward politics. Probably it was the slavery issue, the

Jane Pierce regularly rode in this carriage from the White House to the Capitol where she watched the debates in Congress. The carriage had been presented to the Pierces by the citizens of Boston.

same topic that was fueling fierce debate all over the country.

Jane Pierce had always been a foe of slavery. Now, listening to the arguments that raged in Congress, she opposed it more strongly than ever. Franklin Pierce sought to mend the widening breach between the free North and the slave-holding South. He searched for ways to unite the nation through compromise. His wife, on the other hand, believed the United States should abolish slavery at any cost, even if it meant fighting a civil war.

The most heated debate in Con-

This view of the House of Representatives shows the galleries in which Jane Pierce sat as she listened to the congressional debates regarding the expansion of slavery into the U.S. territories and the new states.

gress involved the expansion of slavery into U.S. territories and new states. Some people felt that only Congress should decide where slavery would be legal. Others wanted the states and the territories themselves to make the choice. President Pierce was one of those who favored "popular sovereignty," giving the states and territories decision-making power.

The Kansas-Nebraska Act was introduced into Congress in 1854. If it passed, the act would let the people of the Kansas and Nebraska Territories choose whether to permit slavery within their borders. Franklin Pierce

This angry exchange in Congress, where tempers often flared over the slavery issue, took place in 1851 between Brown and Wilcox of Mississippi.

took a firm stand in favor of the bill. But Jane Pierce feared it would encourage the expansion of slavery into new lands. Among friends and acquaintances, she spoke out against the act. She argued with her husband, trying to make him change his mind. To her dismay, he signed the bill into law.

A few days after the Kansas-Nebraska Act was signed, Jane received a letter from the wife of Dr. Charles Robinson. Dr. Robinson was an abolitionist, a person who wanted to end slavery forever. Now, he was in prison for helping runaway slaves escape to freedom. Robinson's wife begged the First Lady to help secure

Freedom Train

★ ☆ ★ ☆ ★ ☆ ★ ☆ ★ ☆ ★ ☆ ★ ☆ ★ ☆ ★ ☆ ★ ☆ ★ ☆ ★ ☆ ★ ☆

Dr. Charles Robinson was among many who risked their lives to help runaway slaves escape. A secret network of people called the "Underground Railroad" helped slaves move and hide until they reached safety in the North and Canada. The term came into use when a slave owner, frustrated by his runaway slave, exclaimed, "He must have gone off on some underground road." Soon, slaves all over the South were whispering about the "Underground Railroad." They started using railroad terms: safe houses were "stations" and their owners, "stationmasters." The most dangerous role was that of "conductor." Conductors slipped into the South, helped arrange escapes, and guided slaves ("passengers") along the route to safe stations. The most famous conductor was Harriet Tubman. A slave who ran away on her own, Tubman first sneaked back into the slave states to rescue her sister's family, who were about to be sold. She escorted more than 300 passengers to freedom using such canny tricks as fleeing south to elude slave catchers. Surely no runaways would head *south*! But the Underground Railroad took any route that led to freedom.

Dr. Charles Robinson was an abolitionist who was sent to prison for helping runaway slaves escape to freedom.

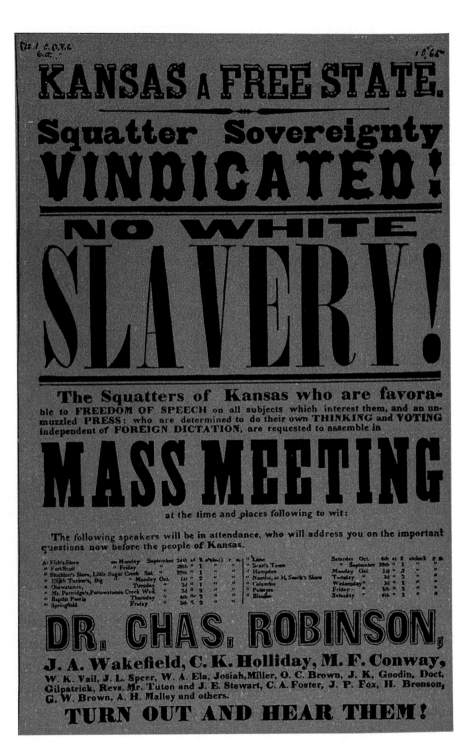

Before the Kansas-Nebraska Act was signed into law, many rallies were held for and against the bill. This poster advertised abolitionist Dr. Charles Robinson as the main speaker at a series of rallies calling for Kansas to be a free state.

his release. Jane asked her husband to do whatever he could on Dr. Robinson's behalf. Within a short time, Dr. Robinson was out of jail.

Jane Pierce was no longer the "shadow in the White House." But she still wore the black of mourning wherever she went. She had not forgotten her aching grief. As one visitor to the White House observed, "Her woebegone face banished all animation in others. She broke down in her efforts to lift herself."

Though she was more visible in public life, Jane was frail and sickly. She may have been in the early stages

Though Jane attended White House receptions like this one during the last two years of her husband's administration, she was not a cheerful presence in her black dresses of mourning.

A full-length portrait of President Franklin Pierce

During the Pierce years, as always, guides led groups

of tourists through the public buildings of Washington, D.C. This group is touring the Capitol.

of tuberculosis, the chronic lung disease that had killed her father. Many people in the capital regarded her as an invalid.

Franklin Pierce had hoped the Kansas-Nebraska Act would resolve the slavery question in a peaceful manner. Instead, it led to a terrible struggle. In Kansas, bitter words turned to gunfire between pro-slavery and anti-slavery factions. As the fighting grew more savage, the territory became known as "Bleeding Kansas." People on both sides put the blame on President Pierce.

As the election of 1856 drew near, it was clear that Franklin Pierce could not win another term as president. The Kansas-Nebraska Act had put an end to his political career. In March 1857, President Pierce and his wife left the White House. It was time to make way for a new president—James Buchanan.

Savage fighting erupted in Kansas after the Kansas-Nebraska Act became law.

James Buchanan was inaugurated president in March 1857.

CHAPTER SIX

Seeking the Cure

☆ ☆ ☆ ☆ ☆ ☆ ☆ ☆ ☆ ☆ ☆ ☆ ☆ ☆

Jane Pierce never had a strong constitution. By the time Buchanan was sworn in as president, her health was more precarious than ever. She was fifty-one years old, and life had treated her harshly. Rumors about Mrs. Pierce's illness flew across Washington. Some people said she was so weak she had to be carried from the White House on a stretcher.

Jane was frail, but she definitely walked out of the White House. She and Franklin spent the next two months in Washington. They visited friends and reveled in being private citizens once more. Then they set out for Concord, New Hampshire, and home.

☆ ☆ ☆ ☆ ☆ ☆ ☆ ☆ ☆ ☆ ☆ ☆ ☆ ☆

The Pierces returned to their home in Concord, New Hampshire, in 1857, two months after Franklin's term as president had ended.

Back in Concord, Jane's condition grew steadily worse. At the time, the only treatment for tuberculosis was a change of climate. Some doctors urged patients to go to the mountains, where they could breathe pure, clean air. Others recommended warm places, especially those near the sea. After many consultations with Jane's physicians, the Pierces set out in search of a cure.

Jane and Franklin Pierce sailed to Europe in the fall of 1857, just in time to avoid the icy New England winter. They spent six months on the lovely Portuguese island of Madeira. When-

The Great White Plague

✶ ✶

One of the deadliest diseases of Jane Pierce's time—and for centuries before—was tuberculosis (TB). Although we know today that TB is caused by bacteria that attacks the lungs and lymph nodes, nineteenth-century doctors knew nothing of bacteria. Powerless to help, they prescribed bed rest and fresh air. However, these were of little effect against the deadly microbe, which can lurk in the body for years before becoming active. Often called "consumption" because the disease consumes and weakens its victims, its symptoms include a severe cough, difficult breathing, and chest pains. People catch tuberculosis by inhaling the bacteria coughed into the air by those infected, and so it was particularly common in the crowded and unsanitary nineteenth-century cities. In those days before pasteurization, many children contracted a type of tuberculosis from contaminated cow's milk. Although Dr. Robert Koch isolated the tubercule bacterium in 1882, it would take another sixty years for someone to discover an antibiotic to cure the disease. Today, drug-resistant strains of TB are beginning to appear, and three million people die of tuberculosis annually around the world.

ever she felt strong enough, Jane walked beside the ocean, enjoying the balmy breezes. But even Madeira's gentle climate failed to improve her health.

In the spring of 1858, the Pierces left Madeira for Spain. For the next year, they visited France, England, and Italy, where they met their old friend Nathaniel Hawthorne. Often they stayed at spas, which are resorts known for the healing powers of water from natural springs. But the most famous spas in Europe failed to restore Jane Pierce's health.

Eventually, Jane and Franklin sailed to the Bahamas. Even on the sunny beaches beneath the palm trees,

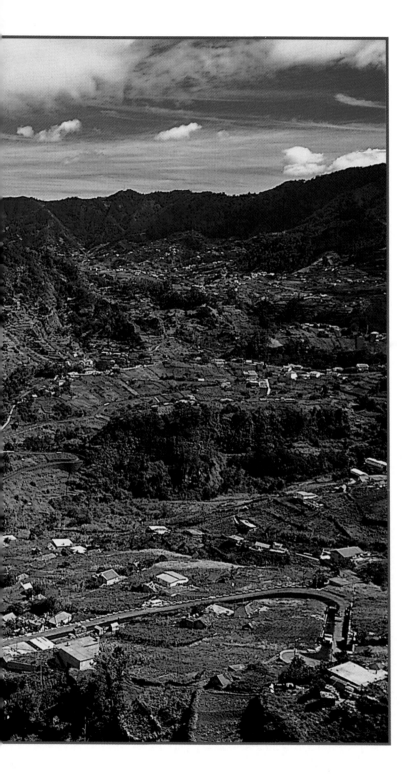

Even six months spent in the gentle climate of the lovely Portuguese island of Madeira failed to improve Jane Pierce's health.

In her travels through Europe searching for a cure, Jane Pierce visited spas like this one in Bath, England. However, the healing powers of water from those natural springs failed to restore her health.

Jane Pierce was not alone in her belief that fresh seaside air might help cure her illness. Throngs of people regularly spent time on Brighton Beach in England for medicinal purposes.

however, Jane Pierce's health continued to fail.

All during her travels, Jane thought of her dead children. She always carried a little box containing locks of their hair. She also kept Bennie's Bible with her wherever she went. She no longer blamed Franklin for Bennie's death. In fact, one of her most cherished possessions was a bracelet her husband gave her on their visit to Rome. It opened like a locket and contained a strand of his hair. Nevertheless, she found it hard to show her affection and tenderness. She once told a friend sadly that she

When Jane's health was still failing after her stay in the Bahamas, she decided it was finally time to return to Concord. She and Franklin had been traveling in search of a cure for more than two years.

Forget Me Not

✴ ✴

During the nineteenth century, hair jewelry became a fashionable way of remembering loved ones, deceased and living. Those in mourning often had elaborate "hairwork" bracelets, pendants, and rings made from the woven hair of the deceased. Delicate goldwork and pearls, representing the tears of the bereaved, sometimes decorated these pieces. Good friends, close relatives, and lovers might exchange jewelry that incorporated a lock of their hair. Over the years, designs became more and more lavish, and woven hair shaped into tubes could be crafted into fragile drop earrings and other three-dimensional forms. Men might sport hairwork watch chains and charms shaped like tiny drums or pistols. No head in history has yielded more hair jewelry, perhaps, than that of George Washington, who frequently gifted friends and relatives with hair mementos. Even his wife's wedding ring included a lock of this famous hair.

Hairwork bracelets like this one were popular in the nineteenth century.

had never learned to open her heart to her husband.

By the spring of 1860, Jane was convinced that she did not have long to live. She was weary of searching for a cure that could not be found. She longed to be near the graves of her children. After more than two years abroad, she and Franklin returned to Concord once more.

Jane's last years were quiet ones. She read and wrote letters, staying in touch with family and friends. When she felt strong enough, she went to church or entertained visitors. Nathaniel Hawthorne and his family remained very close to her. Hawthorne dedicated one of his books, *Our Old Home: A Series of English Sketches,* to Franklin Pierce. In appreciation, Jane wrote to him: "I have too long delayed from ill health and other circumstances to acknowledge your pleasant book, which I have read from beginning to end. . . . The added interest of the preface and the warm assurance of a friendship which has on both sides been so constant, so affectionate, and so true, gives it a [great] hold upon my regard."

Yet Jane could not escape the troubling world beyond Concord's fields and drawing rooms. Tensions over the slavery issue threatened to tear the nation apart. Early in 1861, eleven Southern states seceded from the Union to form a country of their own. Their move triggered the Civil War, the bloodiest conflict in American history.

A decade before, Franklin Pierce had seen war on the horizon. He had worked for compromise between the North and South. Now, he watched young men in blue uniforms gather on Concord's village square to march off to war. Pierce felt that President Abraham Lincoln could have prevented the war from breaking out. He could have found ways to compromise and hold the country together. Nothing was worth this bloodshed.

Weak though she was, Jane held to her own opinion. She supported the war effort if it would put an end to slavery. When she and her husband talked about the fighting, their passions ran high.

While away from home on a short trip, Franklin Pierce wrote to Jane in

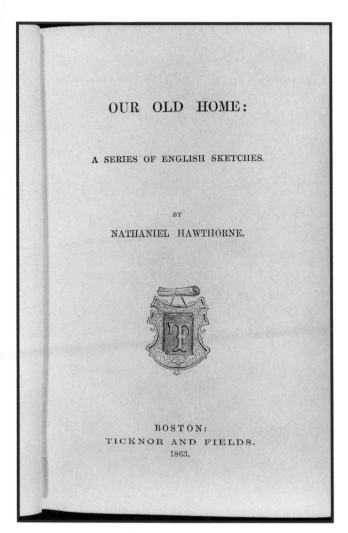

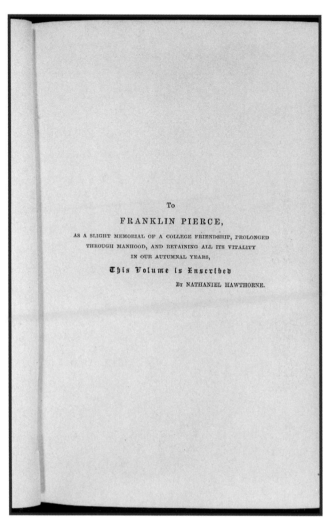

OUR OLD HOME:

A SERIES OF ENGLISH SKETCHES.

BY

NATHANIEL HAWTHORNE.

BOSTON:
TICKNOR AND FIELDS.
1863.

To

FRANKLIN PIERCE,

AS A SLIGHT MEMORIAL OF A COLLEGE FRIENDSHIP, PROLONGED
THROUGH MANHOOD, AND RETAINING ALL ITS VITALITY
IN OUR AUTUMNAL YEARS,

This Volume is Inscribed

By NATHANIEL HAWTHORNE.

American author Nathaniel Hawthorne dedicated this book to his longtime friend Franklin Pierce.

Concord. The letter was dated April 1861, soon after Lincoln declared war.

"My purpose, dearest, is immovably taken. I will never sustain, justify, or in any way uphold the cruel, heartless, aimless, unnecessary war. Madness and imbecility are in the ascendant. I shall not succumb to them, come what may. I have no opinions to retract, no line of action to change."

The Civil War: Fast Facts

WHAT: The War Between the States

WHEN: 1861–1865

WHO: Between the Union (Northern states) and the Confederacy (Southern states)

WHERE: Battles fought as far north as Pennsylvania, south to Florida, and as far west as New Mexico

WHY: Many complicated reasons contributed to the outbreak of civil war. Basic differences between the economies and ways of life in the North and the South led to disagreements over slavery and the power of states versus the federal government. When the Southern states left the Union to form their own government, war soon followed.

OUTCOME: After a devastating loss of American life, Northern and Southern, the Union won the war largely because the South ran out of supplies, men, and energy. Slavery was abolished, and the Confederate states returned to the Union.

Jane Pierce and her husband Franklin had very different opinions about whether the North should challenge the South over the slavery issue. When the South attacked the U.S. Army post at Fort Sumter, South Carolina, on April 12, 1861, however, the Civil War began. President Abraham Lincoln (left) called for Union troops to mobilize.

If Jane replied to that letter from Franklin, her answer has been lost to history.

Late in 1863, Jane Pierce went to visit her relatives in Andover, Massachusetts. She died in Andover on December 2. Her parting words were, "Other refuge have I none."

☆ ☆ ☆ ☆ ☆ ☆ ☆ ☆ ☆ ☆ ☆ ☆ ☆ ☆ ☆

FRANKLIN PIERCE

FOURTEENTH

CHAPTER SEVEN

Last Will and Testament

✶ ✶ ✶ ✶ ✶ ✶ ✶ ✶ ✶ ✶ ✶ ✶ ✶ ✶ ✶

Jane Pierce was laid to rest in Concord Cemetery. She is buried beside her three children. In death, she was united with them at last.

Jane had inherited some money from her relatives. Before she died, she drew up a will, explaining how her property should be divided. Her first bequests show her dedication to spreading the word of God. She gave generous gifts to the American Bible Society, the American Society for Foreign Missions, and the American Colonization Society. Her will stated that these bequests were made "to attest my faith in the Christian religion."

✶ ✶ ✶ ✶ ✶ ✶ ✶ ✶ ✶ ✶ ✶ ✶ ✶ ✶ ✶

Jane Means Appleton Pierce is buried in Concord Cemetery.

After these first three gifts, Jane made bequests to her sister and several of her nieces and nephews. She also left money to two servants whom she explained "have long been hired in my family."

Last of all, Jane Pierce bequeathed the rest of her property to her widowed husband. She wrote that the bequest was his "in full and forever." Her closing words were simple, without flourishes or sentiment. She wrote that she was, "in life and in death, your ever affectionate Jane."

Franklin Pierce

Jane Pierce

★ ★ ★ ★ ★ ★ ★ ★ ★ ★ ★ ★ ★ ★

Portrait of America, 1863: A Nation Divided

✫ ✫ ✫ ✫ ✫ ✫ ✫ ✫ ✫ ✫ ✫ ✫ ✫ ✫ ✫ ✫ ✫ ✫ ✫ ✫

Jane Pierce died quietly in 1863 as the devastating Civil War swirled around her. She would not live to see the resolution of the great conflict between the North and the South. Already, the war had raged on for two years with incredible losses. The year 1863 saw the Battles of Chancellorsville and Chickamauga, and the most infamous of all—Gettysburg. In these three battles alone, more than 115,000 Americans on both sides were killed, wounded, or missing. The most popular songs of the day—"When Johnny Comes Marching Home" and "Just Before the Battle, Mother"—expressed the mixture of patriotism and sorrow that most people felt about this war that pitted American against American.

The year had started with President Abraham Lincoln's Emancipation Proclamation. Although it didn't have the power to free all Southern slaves, the proclamation gave them much-needed hope. Harriet Tubman, a former slave, also gave them hope by leading many slaves to freedom. In 1863, she and her followers set 800 South Carolina slaves free. And, for the first time, black soldiers were formed into regiments to fight for the Union.

In the midst of this national crisis, life went on for America's people. West Virginia, opposed to Virginia's proslavery stance, joined the Union as the thirty-fifth state (including the eleven Southern states that had left the Union). The Arizona and Idaho Territories were created. President Lincoln officially declared the third Thursday of November a holiday called Thanksgiving. The smallest wedding in history occurred in February when 35-inch- (89-cm-) tall Tom Thumb married 32-inch- (81-cm-) tall Lavinia Warren. And the Capitol dome, today a symbol of American liberty and freedom, was completed in Washington.

On November 20, 15,000 people gathered at the Gettysburg Battlefield, still devastated from the vicious fighting there only four months before. They came to dedicate a cemetery to the nation's war dead. President Lincoln rose and spoke the ten moving sentences that would live on as the Gettysburg Address. Concluding that "government of the people, by the people and for the people shall not perish from the earth," Lincoln's words still echo today.

The Battle of Chancellorsville

The Presidents and Their First Ladies

YEARS IN OFFICE			
President	Birth–Death	First Lady	Birth–Death
1789–1797			
George Washington	1732–1799	Martha Dandridge Custis Washington	1731–1802
1797–1801			
John Adams	1735–1826	Abigail Smith Adams	1744–1818
1801–1809			
Thomas Jefferson†	1743–1826		
1809–1817			
James Madison	1751–1836	Dolley Payne Todd Madison	1768–1849
1817–1825			
James Monroe	1758–1831	Elizabeth Kortright Monroe	1768–1830
1825–1829			
John Quincy Adams	1767–1848	Louisa Catherine Johnson Adams	1775–1852
1829–1837			
Andrew Jackson†	1767–1845		
1837–1841			
Martin Van Buren†	1782–1862		
1841			
William Henry Harrison‡	1773–1841		
1841–1845			
John Tyler	1790–1862	Letitia Christian Tyler (1841–1842)	1790–1842
		Julia Gardiner Tyler (1844–1845)	1820–1889
1845–1849			
James K. Polk	1795–1849	Sarah Childress Polk	1803–1891
1849–1850			
Zachary Taylor	1784–1850	Margaret Mackall Smith Taylor	1788–1852
1850–1853			
Millard Fillmore	1800–1874	Abigail Powers Fillmore	1798–1853
1853–1857			
Franklin Pierce	1804–1869	Jane Means Appleton Pierce	1806–1863
1857–1861			
James Buchanan*	1791–1868		
1861–1865			
Abraham Lincoln	1809–1865	Mary Todd Lincoln	1818–1882
1865–1869			
Andrew Johnson	1808–1875	Eliza McCardle Johnson	1810–1876
1869–1877			
Ulysses S. Grant	1822–1885	Julia Dent Grant	1826–1902
1877–1881			
Rutherford B. Hayes	1822–1893	Lucy Ware Webb Hayes	1831–1889
1881			
James A. Garfield	1831–1881	Lucretia Rudolph Garfield	1832–1918
1881–1885			
Chester A. Arthur†	1829–1886		

† wife died before he took office   ‡ wife too ill to accompany him to Washington   * never married

1885–1889			
Grover Cleveland	1837–1908	Frances Folsom Cleveland	1864–1947
1889–1893			
Benjamin Harrison	1833–1901	Caroline Lavinia Scott Harrison	1832–1892
1893–1897			
Grover Cleveland	1837–1908	Frances Folsom Cleveland	1864–1947
1897–1901			
William McKinley	1843–1901	Ida Saxton McKinley	1847–1907
1901–1909			
Theodore Roosevelt	1858–1919	Edith Kermit Carow Roosevelt	1861–1948
1909–1913			
William Howard Taft	1857–1930	Helen Herron Taft	1861–1943
1913–1921			
Woodrow Wilson	1856–1924	Ellen Louise Axson Wilson (1913–1914)	1860–1914
		Edith Bolling Galt Wilson (1915–1921)	1872–1961
1921–1923			
Warren G. Harding	1865–1923	Florence Kling Harding	1860–1924
1923–1929			
Calvin Coolidge	1872–1933	Grace Anna Goodhue Coolidge	1879–1957
1929–1933			
Herbert Hoover	1874–1964	Lou Henry Hoover	1874–1944
1933–1945			
Franklin D. Roosevelt	1882–1945	Anna Eleanor Roosevelt	1884–1962
1945–1953			
Harry S. Truman	1884–1972	Bess Wallace Truman	1885–1982
1953–1961			
Dwight D. Eisenhower	1890–1969	Mamie Geneva Doud Eisenhower	1896–1979
1961–1963			
John F. Kennedy	1917–1963	Jacqueline Bouvier Kennedy	1929–1994
1963–1969			
Lyndon B. Johnson	1908–1973	Claudia Taylor (Lady Bird) Johnson	1912–
1969–1974			
Richard Nixon	1913–1994	Patricia Ryan Nixon	1912–1993
1974–1977			
Gerald Ford	1913–	Elizabeth Bloomer Ford	1918–
1977–1981			
James Carter	1924–	Rosalynn Smith Carter	1927–
1981–1989			
Ronald Reagan	1911–	Nancy Davis Reagan	1923–
1989–1993			
George Bush	1924–	Barbara Pierce Bush	1925–
1993–			
William Jefferson Clinton	1946–	Hillary Rodham Clinton	1947–

Jane Means
Appleton Pierce Timeline

1804	★	Lewis and Clark expedition to the Pacific Coast begins in present-day St. Louis, Missouri
		Thomas Jefferson is reelected president
		Franklin Pierce is born
1805	★	Meriwether Lewis has his first glimpse of the Rocky Mountains
1806	★	Jane Means Appleton is born
		Lewis and Clark expedition returns to St. Louis
1807	★	Importing slaves into the United States is prohibited
1808	★	James Madison is elected president of the United States
1812	★	United States declares war on Great Britain, starting the War of 1812
		James Madison is reelected president
1814	★	British burn Washington, D.C., in War of 1812
		Francis Scott Key writes "The Star-Spangled Banner"
		Treaty of Ghent ends the War of 1812
1815	★	Andrew Jackson defeats the British in the Battle of New Orleans after the War of 1812 had ended
1816	★	James Monroe is elected president
1818	★	United States and Britain agree on a permanent border between the United States and eastern Canada at the 49th parallel
1819	★	United States buys Florida from Spain
1820	★	After the death of the Reverend Dr. Jesse Appleton, the family of Jane Means Appleton moves from Brunswick, Maine, to Amherst, Massachusetts
		Missouri Compromise admits Maine as a free state and Missouri as a slave state
		James Monroe is reelected president

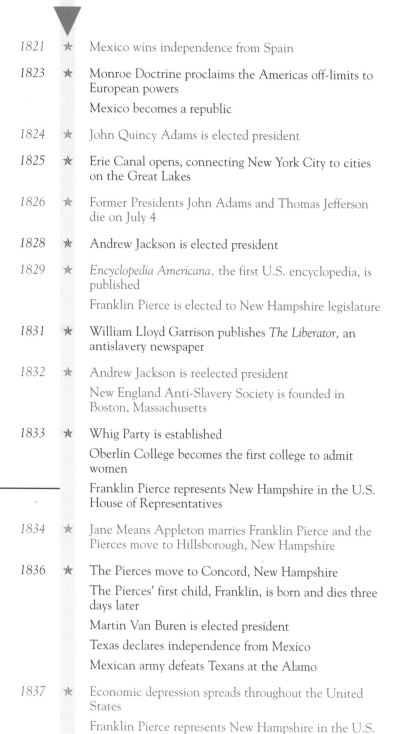

1821	★	Mexico wins independence from Spain
1823	★	Monroe Doctrine proclaims the Americas off-limits to European powers
		Mexico becomes a republic
1824	★	John Quincy Adams is elected president
1825	★	Erie Canal opens, connecting New York City to cities on the Great Lakes
1826	★	Former Presidents John Adams and Thomas Jefferson die on July 4
1828	★	Andrew Jackson is elected president
1829	★	*Encyclopedia Americana,* the first U.S. encyclopedia, is published
		Franklin Pierce is elected to New Hampshire legislature
1831	★	William Lloyd Garrison publishes *The Liberator,* an antislavery newspaper
1832	★	Andrew Jackson is reelected president
		New England Anti-Slavery Society is founded in Boston, Massachusetts
1833	★	Whig Party is established
		Oberlin College becomes the first college to admit women
		Franklin Pierce represents New Hampshire in the U.S. House of Representatives
1834	★	Jane Means Appleton marries Franklin Pierce and the Pierces move to Hillsborough, New Hampshire
1836	★	The Pierces move to Concord, New Hampshire
		The Pierces' first child, Franklin, is born and dies three days later
		Martin Van Buren is elected president
		Texas declares independence from Mexico
		Mexican army defeats Texans at the Alamo
1837	★	Economic depression spreads throughout the United States
		Franklin Pierce represents New Hampshire in the U.S. Senate

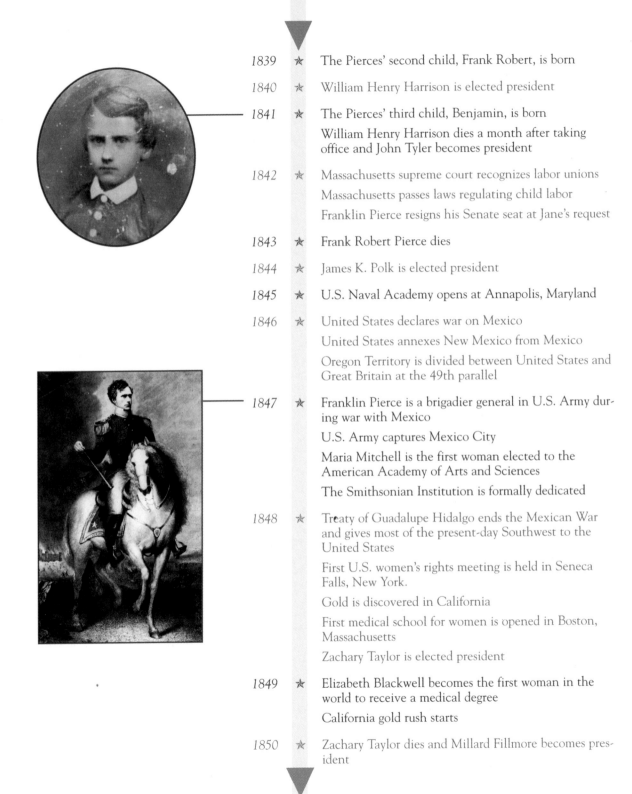

1839	★	The Pierces' second child, Frank Robert, is born
1840	★	William Henry Harrison is elected president
1841	★	The Pierces' third child, Benjamin, is born
		William Henry Harrison dies a month after taking office and John Tyler becomes president
1842	★	Massachusetts supreme court recognizes labor unions
		Massachusetts passes laws regulating child labor
		Franklin Pierce resigns his Senate seat at Jane's request
1843	★	Frank Robert Pierce dies
1844	★	James K. Polk is elected president
1845	★	U.S. Naval Academy opens at Annapolis, Maryland
1846	★	United States declares war on Mexico
		United States annexes New Mexico from Mexico
		Oregon Territory is divided between United States and Great Britain at the 49th parallel
1847	★	Franklin Pierce is a brigadier general in U.S. Army during war with Mexico
		U.S. Army captures Mexico City
		Maria Mitchell is the first woman elected to the American Academy of Arts and Sciences
		The Smithsonian Institution is formally dedicated
1848	★	Treaty of Guadalupe Hidalgo ends the Mexican War and gives most of the present-day Southwest to the United States
		First U.S. women's rights meeting is held in Seneca Falls, New York.
		Gold is discovered in California
		First medical school for women is opened in Boston, Massachusetts
		Zachary Taylor is elected president
1849	★	Elizabeth Blackwell becomes the first woman in the world to receive a medical degree
		California gold rush starts
1850	★	Zachary Taylor dies and Millard Fillmore becomes president

Compromise of 1850 admits California as a free state

Nathaniel Hawthorne's *Scarlet Letter* is published

1851 ⋆ Herman Melville's *Moby Dick* is published

1852 ⋆ Franklin Pierce is elected president

1853 ⋆ Benjamin Pierce dies

Franklin Pierce is inaugurated president of the United States

Jane Means Appleton Pierce moves to the White House

United States acquires the rest of the present-day Southwest through the Gadsden Purchase

1854 ⋆ Republican Party is formed

Kansas-Nebraska Act allows the two territories to decide for themselves whether or not to allow slavery

1856 ⋆ James Buchanan is elected president

1857 ⋆ Pierces return to Concord, New Hampshire

Pierces begin three-year trip to Europe and the Bahamas to restore Jane's health

1858 ⋆ First trans-Atlantic wire is laid between Great Britain and the United States

1860 ⋆ Pierces return to Concord, New Hampshire

Abraham Lincoln is elected president

South Carolina secedes from the Union

1861 ⋆ Confederate States of America (eleven seceded Southern states) is formed

Confederates fire on Fort Sumter, starting the Civil War

1862 ⋆ Confederate army defeats Union forces at the Second Battle of Bull Run and at Fredericksburg

1863 ⋆ President Lincoln issues the Emancipation Proclamation

Union forces defeat the Confederacy in major battles at Gettysburg and Vicksburg

President Lincoln gives the Gettysburg Address

Jane Means Appleton Pierce dies on December 2

Fast Facts about
Jane Means Appleton Pierce

Born: March 12, 1806, in Hampton, New Hampshire

Died: December 2, 1863, in Andover, Massachusetts

Burial Site: Concord Cemetery in Concord, New Hampshire

Parents: Jesse Appleton and Elizabeth Means Appleton

Education: A general education at home that developed a life-long love of reading and writing

Marriage: To Franklin Pierce on November 10, 1834, until her death

Children: Franklin, who died three days after his birth in 1836; Frank Robert (1839–1843); and Benjamin (1841–1853)

Places She Lived: Hampton, New Hampshire (1806–?); Brunswick, Maine (?–1820); Amherst, Massachusetts (1820–1834); Hillsborough, New Hampshire (1834–1836); Concord, New Hampshire (1836–1853, 1857, 1860–1863); Washington, D.C. (1853–1857); Madeira, Spain, Italy, France, England, the Bahamas (1857–1860)

Major Achievements:

★ Because Jane Pierce was in mourning after the death of her son, her aunt, Abby Means, acted as First Lady in her place. On New Year's Day 1855, Jane finally began hosting White House receptions.

★ Watched the debates in Congress regularly from 1854 on.

★ Tried to convince her husband not to sign the Kansas-Nebraska Act (1854) because she felt slavery should be abolished even if it meant Civil War.

★ Asked her husband for help in gaining the release of Dr. Charles Robinson, an imprisoned abolitionist, who was soon let out of jail.

Fast Facts about
Franklin Pierce's Presidency

Term of Office: Elected in 1852; served as the fourteenth president of the United States from 1853 to 1857.

Vice President: William Rufus Devane King (March 24, 1853, to April 18, 1853); after King's death in April 1853, Pierce had no vice president.

Major Policy Decisions and Legislation:

* Signed the Gadsden Purchase (1853), which completed the amount of land the United States controlled in the present-day Southwest.

* Signed the Kansas-Nebraska Act (1854) which set up the territories of Kansas and Nebraska and gave the settlers in each territory the right to decide for themselves if they would allow slavery or not.

* Signed an act that gave U.S. citizenship rights to children whose parents were U.S. citizens but who were born in other countries (1855).

* Sent Congress a message in which he recognized the proslavery government of the Kansas Territory (1856).

* Vetoed nine bills sent from Congress, many of which were for improving rivers for traffic. Congress overrode five of the vetoes.

Major Events:

* Central heating is installed in the White House (1853).

* Pierce gains appointment of John Archibald Campbell as associate justice to the Supreme Court (March 25, 1853).

* First Christmas tree is set up in the White House (1856).

* Pierce presides over the opening of the Crystal Palace Exhibition of Industry of All Nations, the first World Fair held in the United States (July 1853).

Where to Visit

The Capitol Building
Constitution Avenue
Washington, D.C. 20510
(202) 225-3121

Museum of American History of the Smithsonian Institution
"First Ladies: Political and Public Image"
14th Street and Constitution Avenue NW
Washington, D.C.
(202) 357-2008

National Archives
Constitution Avenue
Washington, D.C.
(202) 501-5000

The National First Ladies Library
The Saxton McKinley House
331 South Market Avenue
Canton, Ohio 44702

The Pierce Manse
14 Penacock Street
Concord, New Hampshire 03302-0425
(503) 224-7668

White House
1600 Pennsylvania Avenue
Washington, D.C. 20500
Visitors' Office: (202) 456-7041

White House Historical Association
740 Jackson Place NW
Washington, D.C. 20503
(202) 737-8292

Online Sites of Interest

Concord, New Hampshire, Pierce Manse

http://cityguide-att.lycos.com/newengland/ConcordNH.html

This city site has links to everything of interest in the city, including a photo and description of the Pierce Manse, located in the Concord Historical District

The First Ladies of the United States of America

http://www2.whitehouse.gov/WH/glimpse/firstladies/html/firstladies.html

A portrait and biographical sketch of each First Lady plus links to other White House sites

History Happens

http://www.usahistory.com/presidents

A site that contains fast facts about Franklin Pierce, including personal information and inaugural address

Internet Public Library, Presidents of the United States (IPL POTUS)

http://www.ipl.org/ref/POTUS/fpierce.html

An excellent site with much information on Franklin Pierce, including personal information and facts about his presiden-cy; many links to other sites including biographies and other internet resources

The National First Ladies Library

http://www.firstladies.org

The first virtual library devoted to the lives and legacies of America's First Ladies; includes a bibliography of books, articles, letters, and manuscripts by and about the nation's First Ladies; also includes a virtual tour, with pictures, of the restored Saxton McKinley House in Canton, Ohio, which houses the library

The White House

http://www.whitehouse.gov/WH/Welcome.html

Information about the current president and vice president; White House history and tours; biographies of past presidents and their families; a virtual tour of the historic building, current events, and much more

The White House for Kids

http://www.whitehouse.gov/WH/kids/html/kidshome.html

Includes information about White House kids, past and present; famous "First Pets," past and present; historic moments of the presidency; and much more

For Further Reading

Gormley, Beatrice. *First Ladies*. New York: Scholastic, Inc., 1997.

Gould, Lewis L. (ed.). *American First Ladies: Their Lives and Their Legacy*. New York: Garland Publishing, 1996.

Guzzetti, Paula. *The White House*. Parsippany, N.J.: Silver Burdett Press, 1995.

Klapthor, Margaret Brown. *The First Ladies*. 8th edition. Washington, D.C.: White House Historical Association, 1995.

Mayo, Edith P. (ed.). *The Smithsonian Book of the First Ladies: Their Lives, Times, and Issues*. New York: Henry Holt, 1996.

Paletta, Lu Ann. *World Almanac of First Ladies*. New York: World Almanac, 1990.

Simon, Charnan. *Franklin Pierce*. Encyclopedia of Presidents. Chicago: Childrens Press, 1988.

Skarmeas, Nancy. *First Ladies of the White House*. Nashville, Tenn.: Ideals, 1995.

Index

Page numbers in **boldface type** indicate illustrations

Photo Identifications

Cover: Jane Means Appleton Pierce with her son Bennie
Page 8: The Reverend Dr. Jesse Appleton, Jane's father
Page 18: Franklin Pierce portrait
Page 28: Franklin Pierce as a brigadier general in 1852
Page 44: Jane Means Appleton Pierce in 1852, the year Franklin was elected president
Page 58: President Franklin Pierce portrait
Page 76: Jane Means Appleton Pierce in 1862
Page 90: Franklin Pierce statue on the grounds of the state capitol in Concord, New Hampshire

Photo Credits©

White House Historical Association— Cover, 42, 58
New Hampshire Historical Society— 8 (#4637), 23 (#F859), 28 (#1726), 30 (#D120), 32 (#2819), 44 (#1533), 76 (#3365), 85 (#4629), 87 (#4635 and #4636), 93 (right, #4638), 100 (top, #D120), 101 (#1533)
North Wind Picture Archives— 10, 11, 15, 20, 21 (bottom), 25, 46, 62, 65, 66
Stock Montage, Inc.— 13, 26, 37, 39, 49, 54, 56 (both pictures), 72–73, 89, 95, 98 ; Steve Bruno, 12
Corbis–Bettmann— 16, 17, 18, 21 (top), 22, 24, 31, 36, 38, 47, 52, 60, 63, 67, 69, 72 (left), 74, 75, 82, 83, 93 (left), 99, 100 (bottom); Underwood & Underwood, 92
North Wind Pictures— 35, 40–41, 51, 61, 70, 71, 90
UPI/Corbis-Bettmann— 50, 78
Smithsonian Institution— 53
Tony Stone Images, Inc.— Walter Schmid, 80–81; Rob Boudreau, 84

About the Author

Deborah Kent grew up in Little Falls, New Jersey, and received a B.A. in English from Oberlin College. She earned a master's degree from Smith College School of Social Work and worked for several years at the University Settlement House in New York City. For five years she lived in San Miguel de Allende, Mexico, where she wrote her first novel for young adults.

Ms. Kent is the author of a dozen young-adult novels as well as many titles in the Children's Press America the Beautiful series. *Jane Means Appleton Pierce* is her first title in the Encyclopedia of First Ladies series.

Deborah Kent lives in Chicago with her husband, author R. Conrad Stein, and their daughter Janna.